ROSES IN DECEMBER

Minds, moods, imaginings.

A collection of poems

by Linda Pullman

Roses in December

Linda Pullman

ISBN: 978-1-7397036-0-8

Published by Linda Pullman Publishing in conjunction with Writersworld. This book is produced entirely in the UK, is available to order from most book shops in the United Kingdom and is globally available via UK-based Internet book retailers and www.amazon.com.

Copy edited by Ian Large

Cover design by Jag Lall (www.jaglallart.com)

Image by S. Hermann & F. Richter from Pixabay
Image by suju-foto from Pixabay
Image by Deog Yeon Hwang from Pixabay
Image by Monika Schröder from Pixabay
Photo by Adam Lukac from Pexels

www.writersworld.co.uk

WRITERSWORLD

2 Bear Close Flats, Bear Close, Woodstock,
Oxfordshire, OX20 1JX, United Kingdom
☎ 01993 812500
☎ +44 1993 812500

The text pages of this book are produced via an independent certification process that ensures the trees from which the paper is produced come from well managed sources that exclude the risk of using illegally logged timber while leaving options to use post-consumer recycled paper as well.

Special thanks to present and past members of my writing group, Aylesbury Writers, and to Jan Moran Neil (Creative Ink) for their unerring patience and encouragement during the long drawn-out writing process!

CONTENTS

THE MIND WANDERS

Message from our Mechanics, June 2090

Your mood machine should give you years of service.
Just a little self-assembly is required.
The 'moodal' range is wide
and every nuance is supplied,
from despair to full-on gaiety as desired.

We advise that you should travel slowly,
just one emotional level at a time.
Any bigger step may cause
a temporary pause
and disturb the inner workings of the mind.

Should you reach the over-joyous level quickly
you will find that to sustain it is a chore.
Your colleagues may complain
that your ideas touch insane
and chances of promotion will be poor.

The mood machine will follow your directions,
be they conscious or unconscious, just the same.
If in sleep you choose to slide
down the 'moodal' range supplied,
in the morning you can choose to rise again.

Should your mood machine be faulty on arrival,
please return it with your invoice for exchange.
If a fault develops later
it will be an indicator
that others choose your daily 'moodal' range.

Trading at the Social Skills Exchange, December 2460

Walk this way, ladies and gentlemen.
The Exchange begins trading at ten-thirty
and there's something for everyone.

On your left, you can see the Bright Side.
Stop here to exchange
one compliment for two smiles,
one helping hand for two warm wishes.
In fact, any fair offers will be considered.
Gift wrapping is available for regular customers.

On your right, ladies and gentlemen,
you can see the Dark Side.
Insults are on special offer this week.
Exchange one smirk for two angry words,
one self-rewarding lie for two vicious rumours.
Impress your friends with our new line
in wild, but highly believable excuses.

When your exchanges are complete
please head for the exit,
armed with a battery of new weapons
for *your* social battlefields.

Meeting of the Town Council – Just After Lunch

Mr Chairman and all present,
I bring to your attention the considerable congestion
on all the roads across this busy town.
I propose we forge ahead and build
a ring around our ring road.

Thank you for your input.
So a ring around the ring road is proposed.
Are there any other views or suggestions?

Mr Chairman and all present,
I agree. A massive ring road
is an excellent idea.
But can we not think bigger
and encircle all of England,
not just our little town?

Thank you for your input.
Are there any thoughts on this matter?

Mr Chairman and all present,
what a brilliant suggestion.
We could build it on stilts
to span the mouths of rivers,
an architectural miracle,
the envy of the world.

I second that proposal.
Let's build sky-high escalators
to bring us to the joining points
along the circular route.

Thank you all for your suggestions
but may I now propose a motion
that all members of committee
refrain from drinking brandy after lunch?

The Life Library

Are you finding *you* unexciting?
Are you looking for something radical
to change the way you are?
Come to the Life Library and choose a slice
of another life from our varied selection,
all of them ready to be borrowed.

It's a short-term loan arrangement,
a slice of life, famous or not, for thirty days.
Your present life is stored by us.
We will take care of it, keep it in cellophane,
and protect it from the ageing process.

But should you do a late return
or no return at all, we reserve the right
to lend your life slice
to other clients, as the library
has limited storage.
A full catalogue of life slices
can be viewed at reception.

The Mind Switch Hour

The Mind Switch Hour approaches.
Plans must be made,
taxes paid,
and tickets bought for trains and coaches.
Do not delay.

Are you fully committed, mind and soul?
Have you taken stock?
Is your mind ready to unlock?
It will not roll out of your control
until the Mind Switch Hour.

At the Hour there will be no sudden shock.
The two minds will approach and blend,
co-comprehend.
Your acquired mind will steadily unlock.
Do not be afraid.

Your new mind may oppose your very core
but face it
and embrace it.
Consider those views that you deplore.
It is a learning ground.

Power Up!

Conquering death was momentous.
The World Circuit is on track to power up
all humans in all regions.
Sockets will be upgraded to avoid overload.

All will run smoothly if we remember
to switch ourselves off and pull out the plug
in down times when we don't want to reason
and we have nothing whatsoever to say.

Extension leads and junction boxes will be
issued to carry the heavier loads
in areas of disease, conflict or disaster
and where connections are not yet complete.

On the domestic front, crossed wires are
causing a problem in some areas.
We should try to unravel our thoughts
before we express them on-wire.

Power cuts may frustrate us
or cause unpleasant flashbacks
to the time when death was inevitable.
But as our world expands over its many planets
there is nothing to fear. We are powered,
empowered and connected.

The Friendship Shop, 2022

As big brands desert our high streets,
new enterprises are seizing the opportunity
to take their place.
The world of retail is changing.

One such enterprise is the Friendship Shop
where you can build a new friend from qualities in stock.
Payment will not be required as
commitment is currency.

Their window displays show common friend qualities,
such as listening ears, boxes of favours, lending hands.
Further qualities can be viewed inside
and rarer qualities can be ordered in.

Staff members are highly qualified
in all aspects of friend building and are on hand
should their technical skills be needed
during the building process.

Many customers build likenesses of themselves
but some choose qualities that complement their own.
Those interested in appearances will enjoy using
the holograph machines and 3D printers.

Other ground-breaking enterprises are also doing well
in town centres around the country.
High streets are viable once again
and hopefully will be for many years to come.

The Cheese Wire

It has been confirmed today that our
relocation plan is complete.
We will be detaching our country,
that is, England, Wales and Scotland,
from its deepest roots,
slicing it horizontally with the giant Cheese Wire
and taking it to warmer seas.

Arrangements for Northern Ireland
will take a little longer to complete
owing to a possible imbalance
of the whole island as its
northern section is sliced away.
But hopefully our Irish friends will be able
to join us when this difficulty is resolved.

The giant Cheese Wire will be in its starting position
on the south coast at dawn on the first of January.
A siren will sound and all citizens
must be in their homes or in other buildings
for their own safety. Buffers have been attached
to coastlines to avoid crumbling.

The Cheese wire will glide effortlessly
under the surface, from the south to the north.
There may be an occasional squeak
or scrape as it slices through harder rocks.

When the Wire has completed its work
and our island surface lays loose, the mighty
nuclear engines will fire up and
carry it to its new, warmer resting place.

And lastly, should some of our citizens choose
not to make this journey to warmer seas,
we wish them every success swimming to mainland
Europe
and trust that they will receive a warm welcome.

THE MIND IN TURMOIL

The Agoraphobic's Resolution

I will go into the sunshine but not today.
Today I will order my thoughts
and plan my approach,
raise my objections in alphabetical order
and strive to dismiss them.

I will go out
when the time is right,
when this heavy weight
no longer restricts me
and I can take risks,
knowing that they will not break me.

I will go out
in my own time, not theirs.
I will not be a tick on their form
and I will not count the steps
to comply with their programme.
There will be no tally.

I will go out
when the need to go out
surpasses the fear.
I will know that moment.
They will not choose it.
I will one day fight my demon.

I will go out
and feel the warmth
seeping through my skin
and into my bones.
This place is cold now
in every season.

When I do go out
I will go alone and talk to myself.
I'll tell myself that I am stronger than this,
tell myself that it is possible to go a distance
holding the dread at arm's length
and not counting the steps.

I *will* go out into the sunshine
In my own time.

War Zone

Come out of that rubble, Child.
This is no place to be.
Pick up your feet and follow me.

But I'm tired of walking, Mother.
Can't we stop? The ground is dry.
We could spread the blanket over.
Oh Mother, can't we try?

The dark is closing in, Child.
This is no place to be.
Pick up your feet and follow me.

Can we make a shelter, Mother?
Find some wood to keep us warm?
We can stay inside till morning comes
and then, can we go home?

We will not go back home, Child.
It is not the place to be.
Pick up your feet and follow me.

Where *are* we going, Mother?
Will there be guns there too?
Will the soldiers come and find us?
Are all the stories true?

We'll find a new home soon, Child,
a better place, you'll see.
Pick up your feet and follow me.

Where *is* this new place, Mother?
And can all my friends come too?
Do they know where we're going?
Shall we wait and help them through?

We must travel on alone, Child.
You'll see them when we're free.
Pick up your feet and follow me.

Are those *our* soldiers, Mother?
Is it safe to go this way?
Don't hold my hand so tightly.
I won't run away.

We must run to reach those trees, Child.
Pick up your feet and

Mother?

Held To Account

Tonight the world has stilled.
A year has passed and we are weary.
Our account books must be balanced
and decisions must be made.

Is another planet a viable proposition?
We risk a takeover at any time.
Or shall we just declare we're bankrupt
and close down this troubled human firm?

Our current debts are truly massive,
both to others and to ourselves.
The losses we incur now are colossal
and appear on every page.

But not everything we did was so disastrous.
We supported enterprise around the globe.
At best we made a difference, made a profit.
At worst we only traded pain.

Cash flow has been difficult to master.
Disaster and distress are all around.
We have found some temporary solutions
but long-term strategies are needed now.

If the human firm can't find itself a buyer
and undertakes another tough new year,
we hope that the accounting will be balanced
and we'll master profit, cash flow, loss and pain.

Covid-related Moments

I have those moments now (You have them too perhaps?),
when I'm weary of the views from my windows but then,
in the next breath, I'm thinking that at least I *have*
windows and leafy views.

Or I'm having moments filled with self-obsession, seeing
my lockdown as more terrible than anyone else's but then,
maybe one alone is not a bad number if plus-one is one
you wish wasn't there.

Moments when everybody I know seems distant, far
beyond the statutory two metres, but I also know that one
conversation can adjust that measurement.

Moments when 'How are you?' has a myriad of answers,
none of which is the whole truth, but I carry on asking it
and answering it in the accepted format.

There are moments when home seems like prison,
exercise in the yard but no visitors.

And moments when the world outside seems changed and
dangerous but the real changes are in us and how we see it
now.

I have moments when getting up is the greatest trial of the
day but the grass needs cutting, the dog needs feeding and
any day is better than none.

There are moments when boredom and anxiety co-exist. The two lay in waiting for a spark of enthusiasm or purpose and that may take a while.

Digging Deep

They're building a railway.
They're digging a tunnel
just down the end of our garden.

They'll chop down our trees,
an apple and a cherry,
just down the end of our garden.

They've found us a flat.
It's just up the road
but it's not down the end of our garden.

We're not moving Grandad.
He planted the trees
just down the end of our garden.

He tended those trees
through sixty-odd years,
just down the end of our garden.

We won't dig up Grandad.
We'll bury him deeper,
just down the end of our garden.

THE MIND CONNECTS

The Extraordinary Bridge Building Company

We span chasms.
We can connect you.
Although the span may be enormous,
show us the two banks,
the two opposing positions
and we will create the bridge,
material or ethereal.
We have the means.

We can connect you,
nation to nation,
family to family,
lost soul to lost soul.
Come to us when conflict looms
and we will seek
to find solutions that will suit you.

Pay us with your gratitude
and with promises that compromise.
Go forward with confidence,
knowing that all things are linked.
We can connect you.

From the Life-structuring Departure Lounge, February 3030

The queues have been particularly long of late.
Life-structuring is becoming popular.

Today we take neglected mothers.
We have many good family units
in which to place them.
They will have the daughters and sons of their dreams
and partners who come home at night.

Many more family units
are under construction.
Yesterday we took
our monthly batch of misunderstood mothers-in-law,
always over-subscribed.

Tomorrow we will take estranged fathers
who will see their children grow up nearby
and not more than a day away.
They will do more than Sunday visits
and 'spoiling' weekends in toy shops and burger bars.
Their children will not need to pick sides.

At weekends we will take the distressed and the lonely.
Weekends are the worst times, they tell us.
The distressed will believe that time can heal
and the lonely will no longer live in the silence that
oppresses.
They will make meaningful connections.

We have great hopes for the future.
Other planets may serve as re-structuring locations
in less than a year from now.
All current family units are operationally sound
and transfers are secure.
When will *you* try re-structuring?

Social History Museum, Planet 19, a hundred years from now

Welcome, ladies and gentlemen, to the Planet Earth Gallery.
The glass dome you see here is our 2015 Eartharium,
a working model of daily life on Earth,
five years before the start of the COVID-19 pandemic.

Look closely at how urgently Man scuttles, walks and runs
in frantic rounds of chaotic travel, whilst staring down
at a small handheld metal box that talks to him.
He dodges huge moving boxes of metal and glass.

Do you see how Man gathers in brick and stone boxes
of various shapes and sizes with little space between them?
And how he ventures out of these boxes, not looking to left or right,
not acknowledging those who gather in neighbouring boxes?

Other excessively tall brick boxes have many levels
and groups who gather in these boxes must use lifts
to gain access to outside areas and breathe more easily.
Long periods of bad weather restrict this access.

Man becomes unwell frequently and depends on
various emergency services to take him to
enormous brick and glass boxes labelled 'H'.
These are vastly overcrowded, trying to keep Man alive.

Many other species inhabit Earth at this time.
A large number are far faster and stronger than Man.
But he traps them as he traps Himself, stealing their habitats.
He rarely chooses to celebrate their strengths.

Now step this way and you see our 2030 Eartharium,
'The re-structuring of planet Earth, post COVID-19.'
You notice that now Man does not pass his neighbour in haste.
He averts his eyes from his small metal box and he greets him.

The huge boxes now glide almost silently,
emitting no dust or smoke to irritate Man's fragile senses.
They no longer enter the busy, urban areas
so Man can roam in safety and not in fear.

You will notice that those excessively tall boxes
have been removed, making way for more smaller ones,
surrounded by open green areas and cleaner air.
Improved breathing conditions are now common.

The boxes labelled 'H' are no longer overcrowded
as those who are mildly unwell are visited
in their own boxes by their local doctors.
Visits to 'H' are reserved for dire circumstances.

Man now tries to preserve habitats
and live alongside Earth's animal kingdom.
He respects their right to survive
and no longer hunts them down.

As you see, this was a time of great change in Earth's history
when Man took notice of the devastation around him,
stepped up and improved his planet's future.
He created what can justifiably be called a social revolution.

Spaceship Returning to Earth in the Year 3000

We'll have landed by tonight
but the flags will not be flying
as the world will be denying
that catastrophe's in view.

Leaders tell us we are wrong,
that this sphere will not stop spinning
and we won't need a new beginning
on another planet soon.

World leaders must decide
as the darkness is descending
if this Earth-life now is ending
and we need to flee our homes.

So if we shudder to a halt
before they have decided,
we trust that you'll be guided
by the evidence we hold.

If you sense that something's wrong
and your life starts to unravel
do not hesitate to travel
to your micro launching pads.

The second planet's ready
for this massive re-location
of every single nation
and the future is assured.

Could it Happen?

They fetched in more scaffolding to support all the tunnelling
that criss-crossed below the shuddering town.
The sandstone-like caves carved out in pre-history
were threatening to disintegrate deep down in the Earth.
Sink holes were sinking faster and increasing in diameter.
Articulated lorries could almost fall through.

The mayor blamed Planning and Planning blamed Finance.
Finance blamed the government for the sad lack of funds.
The townsfolk blamed the Rail Board for digging excess tunnels
and the Rail Board blamed the building firms for digging too deep.

If only they'd all stopped tunnelling when they heard the rumbling
and listened to the archaeologists who checked out the site.
With just minutes to spare the town was evacuated,
leaving Fire and Rescue to fight to the end.
As the last pole gave way with an ominous clattering
the whole of the town sank down into sand.

And now if you stand on the edge of that sandpit
I swear you can decipher the arguments still.
The mayor blaming Planning and Planning blaming Finance.
Finance blaming the government for the sad lack of funds.

The town has been re-located. It's now on firm foundations
and all underground services are totally banned.

Two Women, Two Lives

Yellow Dress, large red handbag,
gold earrings, stiletto heels.
No seats free, no spaces
on the five o'clock train,
again!

Large red handbag getting heavy.
Puts it down, tight behind her.
Dreams of supper, dreams of rest.
Getting weary on her feet.
Long day!

Black Dress, no earrings,
flat shoes, similar red handbag
wedged beside her by the door
on the five o'clock train
that day.

Whistle sounds. Train tunnels,
rattling, rocking into darkness.
Yellow Dress stumbles. Touches handbag.
Touch feels different.
Not her bag!

Out of tunnel. Black Dress nowhere!
Yellow Dress searches through the carriage.
No-one's seen her. No-one knows her.
Getting frantic on her feet.
Not today!

Train brakes slowly into station.
Stops. Doors open. Yellow Dress
searches platform. Getting worried.
Glimpses Black Dress.
Gone!

Yellow Dress, wrong red handbag.
Dashes up steps. Stiletto heels
send her tumbling. Twisted ankle.
Can't stand on it.
Ouch!

Black Dress, wrong red handbag.
Doesn't notice. Home to dinner.
Daughter questions, 'New handbag?'
Black Dress sees
now!

Black Dress opens wrong handbag.
Places hand in – pulls out gun!
Daughter screams. Black Dress drops it.
Steps away,
stunned!

Meanwhile, Yellow Dress gets up,
Staggers forward. Mounting anger
overcomes her. Husband's safe now
for tonight.
Damn!

Start Dates Saga

I called in a plumber last Monday
when the pipes began to leak.
He said he'd do a temporary fix
and do the rest of the job Friday week.

I called in a carpenter last Tuesday
to replace rotten floorboards with new.
'I can hammer a nail or two now, love,' he said,
'And finish in a week or two.'

I called in a painter last Thursday,
knowing I'd have to wait.
He said he'd put me on his urgent list
and get back in two months with a date.

I called in a roofer last Friday.
He said, 'Blimey, you've got problems here.
We'll cover it up as best we can
and finish it off next year.'

I called an all-round expert on Saturday
whose experience I never questioned.
He climbed in his cab and he bulldozed that house
in less than sixty seconds!

The Writers' Road Services Ltd.

Is your story due for its MOT?
Is your script in need of repair?
Just bring it to us for a service.
Our prices are more than fair.

We'll locate inconsistencies,
get your adjectives under control.
We'll find those pesky plot holes
and seal them once and for all.

We specialise in synonyms.
Speedfix has nothing on us.
We'll replace them if they're faulty
with quality parts that you can trust.

We won't remove your 'darlings'.
We know you love them dearly.
Please don't forget to point them out.
Just underline them clearly.

We stock most kinds of endings
that bolt on, if that's what you seek.
The twist is a very popular choice
or the cliffhanger's on special this week.

Should you publish your serviced work
and it reaches fame's dizzy heights,
we only ask for a small percentage
of all its worldwide rights.

Sale – the Rooms of a Mind

Step this way, Sir. I'll just close the door behind you.
You are looking at the spacious hall of the mind.
There's plenty of room to store your thoughts here
until you need them or choose to discard them.

Just one hall window, as you see. It will remain closed
in early years but it will begin to open as time passes,
allowing some unchecked thoughts to escape.

And here's the classic kitchen diner,
the hub of the house as they say on daytime TV.
A very popular choice as many of you multi-task here,
cooking up ideas and serving them whilst calming
the endless chatter. There is no rest in this room.

Now for the lounge. This is a very different story.
Here you can let your mind relax. You may drift into
the fantasy of the large screen on the wall but
don't keep your mind there for long periods.
You are more than it can show you.
The bookcases carry the thoughts of many minds.
Its books on numerous subjects can be read at your leisure.
There are a number of storage units for your
older memory files, should you wish to keep them.

So let's go back through the hall and up the grand staircase.
You will have noticed the large mirrors. They will be useful to check
if your outward image matches your inner one.
And here, we have the master bedroom complete with
a dressing room of disguises. You'll need these from time to time.
Telling the whole truth can be hurtful. The other two bedrooms
are quite small but adequate for a growing family.

Follow me down into the conservatory, the hothouse of new ideas.
Lap up the sunshine and positivity to your heart's content.
But if sometimes you feel burned by the piercing of the sun's rays
you can adjust the blinds to suit your mood.

Should this property suit your needs and you would like
to put in an offer, our agents at Hodges Home Truths
will be most pleased to represent you.

The Mood Election

On the eve of the annual election,
here is a summary of the parties represented.
You have two votes.

Let's start with the party called 'On the Plate'.
For those in a hurry or lacking in patience.
Relax.
Do nothing.
There will be no need for debate.

The 'Watch Out!' party is for the ever alert.
You never know what may go wrong.
Stay focused.
On guard!
Those under stress may be drawn to vote for this party.

The 'In Your Own Time' party is a leisurely affair.
You can adopt a slower pace of life.
Take time.
Just chill.
No-one will rush you but you know you'll get there.

Will the 'Glass Half Full' party work for you?
If you trust that every cloud has a silver lining,
go forth.
See the good
and open a dark cloud or two.

On your ballot paper, put two ticks only
and be true to yourself.
Choose well
and good luck.
It'll be a long year if you don't like the mix!

I am the Time Keeper

I give and take
the hours and minutes
according to your needs.

In your childhood years,
I give you longer days,
near endless summers.

In your teenage years,
your days stretch into night.
Late mornings follow.

In your middle years,
you try time adjustment for yourself
and call it time management.

In your later years, you carry time
with pride or pain or both, treasuring the moment
or wishing it away.

I give and take
the hours and minutes
until time is called.

THE MIND DREAMS

Soul to Body, Heaven to Earth

Good morning, pre-life class.
Your births are fast approaching.
Group A will embark shortly.
Please collect your Life-Navs from Downloading
before three. They have been
updated,
collated, and
validated
for your journey to Earth.
Please then hurry to your departure gate.
The Birth Train will not wait.

On reaching your destination,
let your Life-Nav guide you to your birth carrier
wherever she may be.
The process of delivery can be messy.
Grasp the screaming baby with conviction
and enter into it. It is yours. It *is you!*
Take it,
respect it,
protect it,
and you will live well.

Your childhood plan is largely pre-formed
and includes your dreams for the future.
We hope that a few of those dreams
will stagger past your teenage years,
take root,
and bear fruit.
Own this body reserved for you.

Should your first carrier falter in early years
you will be given a second carrier
labelled 'friend', 'mentor' or 'protector'.
Do not fret. You will not be alone.

Self-assembly will be needed for the following years
and toolboxes will be available
but you are the builder.
We wish you luck and await your return
in a century or two.

Cradle-rocking 1

I needed her baby,
just for a while.
I needed him so much more than she did.
He's the baby I never had, never will have.

My child waits,
nestling in the corners of my brain,
rocking deep in my mind,
shrivelling, dying, alone and afraid.

Why are you taking me away?
Am I to be punished for wanting a child
and taking it, letting this baby's screams
fuse with those of the baby in my head,
giving life to my child,
for just a while?

I can see the disgust in your eyes.
I never wanted this.
Take me away then if you must.
I have no strength left to fight you now.
Take me to a place where no babies cry
and no mothers rock babies.

Cradle-rocking 2

She took my baby
and I touched hell that afternoon.
It seemed that she had torn me open
and snatched my very core,
causing a cruel, violent, second birth.

As minutes became hours,
I imagined my baby's cold, limp body
far away in this woman's iron arms
as she rocked him to death.
I imagined lifting up his limp body
and fusing it with mine for ever.

And you want me to tell this woman
that I can forgive her?
To tell her that I'm trying to understand.
In that one afternoon
the extremes of love and hate
collided in my brain.
Perhaps one day I *will* speak to this woman
and ask her – why?

Emily is five today

I would give her, if I could,
a life that is not driven
and the knowledge that she has nothing to prove.
She is complete in her incompleteness.

I would give her the capacity to love in degrees,
not in extremes,
and a mind that can be still.
She would have enough pride to stand her ground
when necessary but not enough to destroy.
She would have satisfaction in her achievements
and the acceptance of failure as a learning process.

On this day, I would gift her all-listening ears
to protect her, to warn her of any dangers ahead
and the courage to be herself, to know
that wherever she is, there her home will be.

Roses in December

The December afternoon is darkening now
as the Life-Swap hour approaches,
at breakneck speed, it seems to me.
At ninety Life-Swaps old
I am weary of change and want to rest
in this quiet corner, admiring the roses.
Is that too much to ask?

I have accepted each of my Life-Swap years,
carried them out with no complaint,
ninety lives, each one of ninety years.
Whether I was the bully or the victim,
the accuser or the accused,
the loved or the unloved,
I knew that every life I led
was part of Your Plan.

The afternoon grows ever darker
and the Life-Swap hour is imminent.
Ninety different lives have brought me here.
And actually, I was wondering
if I might stop my journeying now,
make this my final resting place
and smell the roses?

Defences

Brick on brick I built these walls around me,
silently patrolled them night and day.
My castle or my prison I'm defending
against who or what it's difficult to say.

One fine day I'll fashion me some windows,
vast, painted glass in blue and red and gold.
But for now I'll see the world through narrow vistas,
guarded, one-way viewpoints, safe but cold.

I wonder, are we all in prison-castles
or do some prefer to walk the open plains?
And is there two-way journeying between them?
Are we so very different, yet the same?

PRINTED AND BOUND BY:
Copytech (UK) Limited trading as Printondemand-worldwide,
9 Culley Court, Bakewell Road, Orton Southgate.
Peterborough, PE2 6XD, United Kingdom.